T0378977

COUNTRIES OF THE WORLD

Japan

by Rebecca Sabelko

BELLWETHER MEDIA • MINNEAPOLIS, MN

Blastoff! Readers are carefully developed by literacy experts to build reading stamina and move students toward fluency by combining standards-based content with developmentally appropriate text.

Level 1 provides the most support through repetition of high-frequency words, light text, predictable sentence patterns, and strong visual support.

Level 2 offers early readers a bit more challenge through varied sentences, increased text load, and text-supportive special features.

Level 3 advances early-fluent readers toward fluency through increased text load, less reliance on photos, advancing concepts, longer sentences, and more complex special features.

★ **Blastoff! Universe**

Reading Level

 Grade **K**

 Grades **1–3**

 Grade **4**

This edition first published in 2023 by Bellwether Media, Inc.

No part of this publication may be reproduced in whole or in part without written permission of the publisher. For information regarding permission, write to Bellwether Media, Inc., Attention: Permissions Department, 6012 Blue Circle Drive, Minnetonka, MN 55343.

Library of Congress Cataloging-in-Publication Data

Names: Sabelko, Rebecca, author.
Title: Japan / by Rebecca Sabelko.
Description: Minneapolis, MN : Bellwether Media, [2023] | Series: Blastoff! Readers : Countries of the world | Includes bibliographical references and index. | Audience: Ages 5-8 | Audience: Grades 2-3 | Summary: "Relevant images match informative text in this introduction to Japan. Intended for students in kindergarten through third grade" Provided by publisher.
Identifiers: LCCN 2022018174 (print) | LCCN 2022018175 (ebook) | ISBN 9781644877227 (library binding) | ISBN 9781648347689 (ebook)
Subjects: LCSH: Japan–Juvenile literature.
Classification: LCC DS806 .S23 2023 (print) | LCC DS806 (ebook) | DDC 952–dc23/eng/20220420
LC record available at https://lccn.loc.gov/2022018174
LC ebook record available at https://lccn.loc.gov/2022018175

Editor: Elizabeth Neuenfeldt   Designer: Gabriel Hilger

Printed in the United States of America, North Mankato, MN.

Table of Contents

All About Japan

Tokyo

Japan is a country in Asia.
It has more than 6,000 islands!

Tokyo is Japan's capital. It is the most **populated** city in the world!

N
W E
S

Tokyo, Japan

Land and Animals

Japan is covered in forested mountains. Many of the mountains are **volcanoes**. Mount Fuji is the tallest!

Large cities cover the coastal **plains**. Farms dot the countryside.

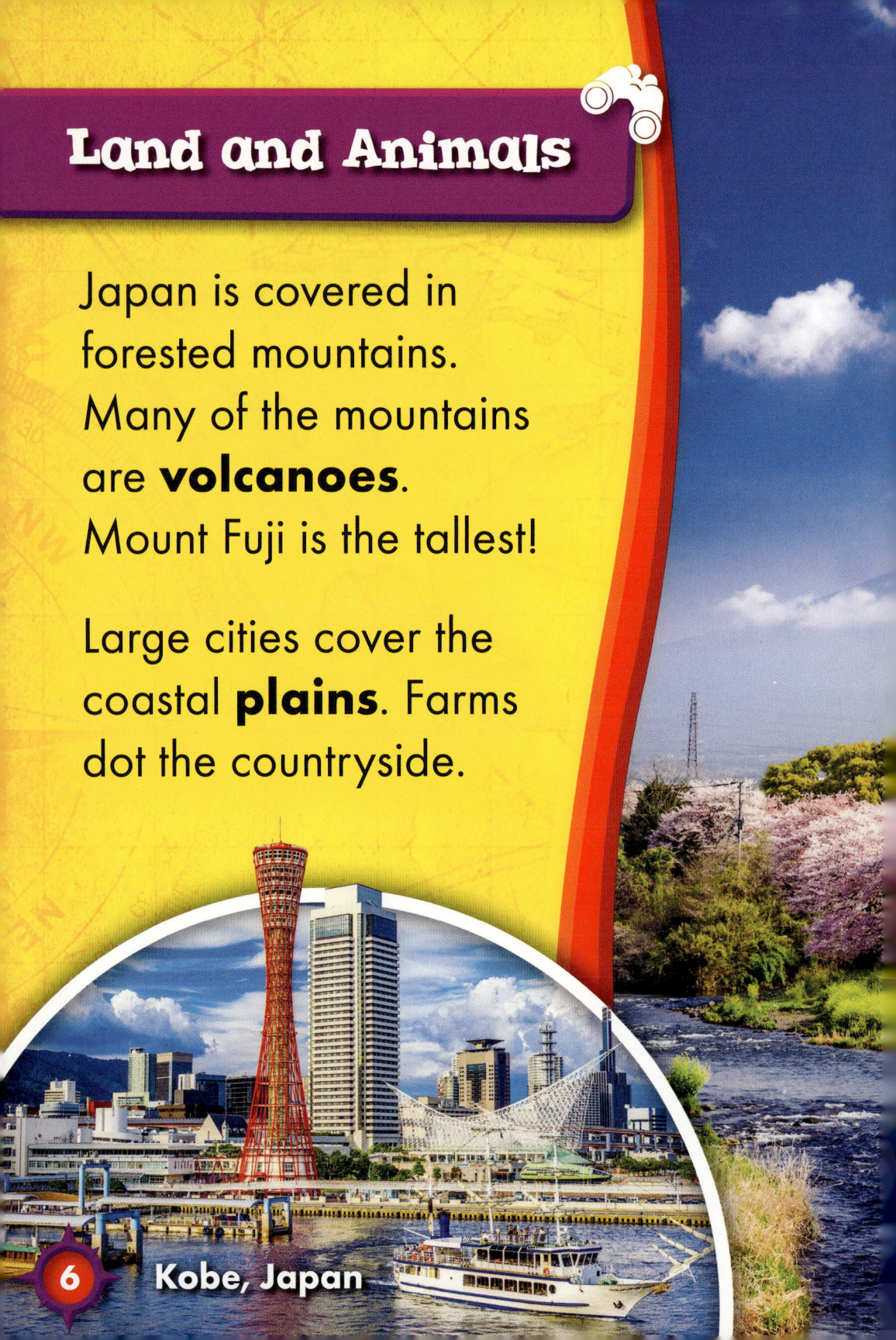

Kobe, Japan

Mount Fuji

Size: 12,388 feet (3,776 meters) tall

Famous For:

- active volcano
- tallest mountain in Japan

Japan has four seasons.
Northern Japan is colder
than southern Japan.

Earthquakes are common. They can bring **tsunamis** from the ocean.

result of an earthquake and tsunami

Black bears live in the mountains.
Snow monkeys rest in **hot springs**.

snow monkeys
in a hot spring

10

Asiatic
black bear

snow monkey

sea eagle

manta ray

Eagles fly above the
Pacific Ocean. Rays swim
in coastal waters.

11

Life in Japan

Most people in Japan have an Asian background. Japanese is the main language.

Most people practice **Shintoism** and **Buddhism**.

Buddhist temple

12

Japanese people enjoy many outdoor activities. They like to ski or visit parks.

14

Baseball is a favorite among sports fans. **Sumo wrestling** is popular, too.

baseball

sumo wrestling

Rice is a **staple** food in Japan.
Miso soup is a tasty dish.

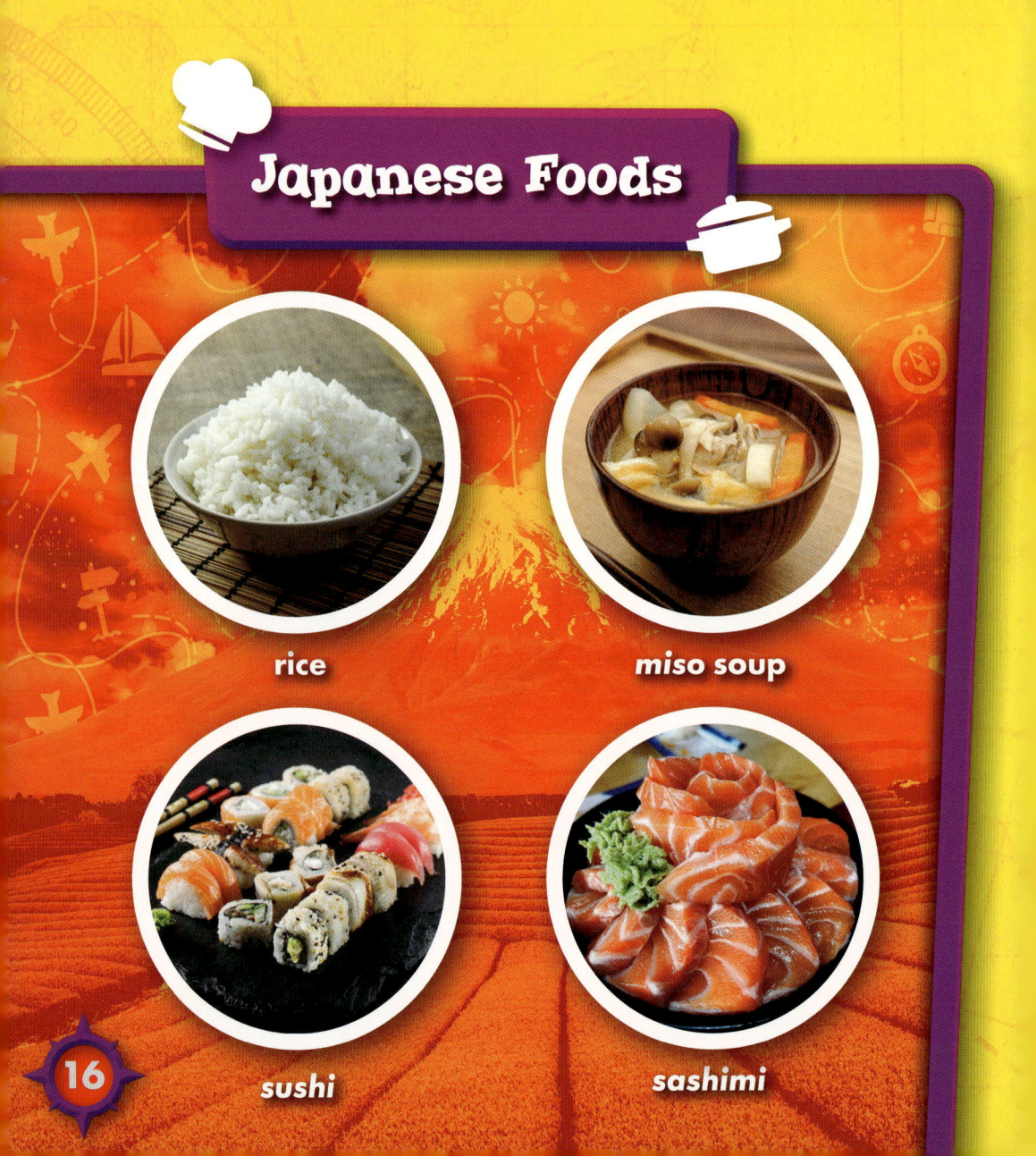

Japanese Foods

rice

miso soup

sushi

sashimi

making *sushi*

Sushi is popular. *Sashimi* is eaten on special occasions. It is thinly cut uncooked fish.

Children's Day
carp streamers

Japan has many holidays.
May 5 is Children's Day.
Families fly carp streamers.
They give children strength.

The Lantern **Festival** welcomes spirits of the dead. Japanese people honor their **traditions**!

19

Japan Facts

Size:
145,914 square miles
(377,915 square kilometers)

Population:
124,214,766 (2022)

National Holiday:
The Emperor's Birthday (February 23)

Main Language:
Japanese

Capital City:
Tokyo

Famous Face

Name: Hayao Miyazaki

Famous For: an award-winning filmmaker, animator, and manga artist

Religions

Christian: 2%

other: 6%

Shinto and/or Buddhist: 92%

Top Landmarks

Arashiyama Bamboo Grove

Itsukushima Shrine

Shibuya Crossing

Glossary

Buddhism—a religion of eastern and central Asia based on the teachings of Buddha, the founder of Buddhism

earthquakes—sudden movements of the earth's crust

festival—a time or event of celebration

hot springs—places where warm water flows out of the ground

plains—large areas of flat land

populated—having people living in a place

Shintoism—a religion created in Japan in which believers follow many gods and spirits

staple—a widely used food or other item

sumo wrestling—a Japanese form of wrestling in which wrestlers try to stay in the ring and keep the bottoms of their feet on the ground

traditions—customs, ideas, or beliefs handed down from one generation to the next

tsunamis—powerful ocean waves caused by earthquakes or underwater volcanoes

volcanoes—holes in the earth; when a volcano erupts, hot ash, gas, or melted rock called lava shoots out.

To Learn More

AT THE LIBRARY

Adamson, Thomas K. *Baseball*. Minneapolis, Minn.: Bellwether Media, 2020.

Dean, Jessica. *Japan*. Minneapolis, Minn.: Pogo, 2019.

Gibbons, Gail. *Volcanoes*. New York, N.Y.: Holiday House, 2021.

ON THE WEB

 FACTSURFER

Factsurfer.com gives you a safe, fun way to find more information.

1. Go to www.factsurfer.com.

2. Enter "Japan" into the search box and click 🔍.

3. Select your book cover to see a list of related content.

Index

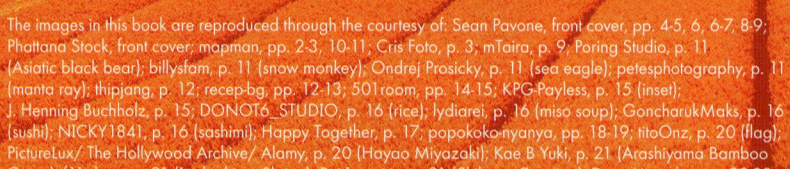